POTTERY WORKERS
IN STAFFORDSHIRE

By the same author in this series:

Stafford and District

Stone and District

Tamworth and District

The Haywoods

S.B. Publications publish a wide range of local interest titles in this series,
For a full list of titles available write (enclosing S.A.E.) to:–

S.B. Publications, c/o 19 Grove Road, Seaford, East Sussex BN25 1TP.

POTTERY WORKERS
IN STAFFORDSHIRE

A PORTRAIT IN OLD PICTURE POSTCARDS

Roy Lewis

S.B. Publications

This book is dedicated to Trevor and Karen Lewis
and their children Emma, Jenny and James.

First published in 1995 by S.B. Publications,
c/o 19 Grove Road, Seaford, East Sussex BN25 1TP

ISBN 1 85770 083 X

Typeset, printed and bound by MFP Design & Print,
Longford Trading Estate, Thomas Street, Stretford, Manchester M32 0JT.

CONTENTS

INTRODUCTION

This book reproduces a selection of picture postcards showing people at work on the potbanks in the Potteries. All the postcards were first published between 1900 and 1960 so they show only the beginnings of the changes that have transformed the pottery industry since World War Two.

The cards have been arranged to follow the stages of manufacture. Those showing the preparation of raw materials are followed by cards showing how cups, saucers, plates, jugs, and sanitary ware were made, fired, and glazed. Next come cards showing how pieces were decorated. The book ends with warehouses, packing sheds, and workers going home to dinner.

The earliest postcards showing work on the potbanks date from 1902 when Reynolds Amor of Alsager published seven views of Wedgwood's works at Etruria in his Roma (Amor reversed) series. These were later reprinted by Wedgwood with the addition of an eighth card showing a statue of Josiah Wedgwood.

In the following years Raphael Tuck & Sons published a set of six cards showing an unidentified works in the Potteries. Various photographs can also be found which were not taken for public sale but were printed with a postcard back. These include views of Twyford's first taken several years earlier to illustrate a guide book by Joseph Hatton. However, the most prolific publishers of postcards of the potbanks at this time were William Blake and William Shaw.

William Blake set up in business as a stationer in Stafford Street, Longton, about 1900. He was also a photographer and took many local views, including a number showing workers in some of the smaller works. A "Potter's Series" of twelve cards from his negatives was published in 1904 and he also supplied negatives to William Shaw. Blake himself published a considerable number of photographic cards and before 1914 these included a number showing workers and processes of manufacture. From 1915 to about 1940 each of his cards was given a number prefaced by the letter B. These include a number of cards showing pottery workers in the 1920s and 1930s

William Shaw of Burslem opened his fancy goods warehouse late in 1904 and began to publish postcards from negatives he had bought from Blake and others. In 1912, but using 1910 photographs, he published a set of twelve cards showing pottery workers on unidentified potbanks and followed this with at least five further groups of cards at intervals into the 1930s. He also published a number of single cards showing pottery workers. Each group is a mixture of reprints and hitherto unpublished photographs. This, added to the fact that the negatives might be up to ten years old when first used, makes dating the scenes shown on Shaw's postcards very uncertain.

In the early 1920s Wedgwood published a series of about forty postcards showing people at work at Etruria. These cards are all in the format shown on pages 36 and 50 but, apart from these two, the illustrations have been enlarged and reproduced without the accompanying text. These photographs were also used to illustrate a Wedgwood handbook written by Harry Barnard.

Shelley Potteries Ltd of Longton published an illustrated booklet, "The Oldest Craft in the World", in the 1950s. All the photographs in it can also be found as postcards. These are the most recent postcards reproduced in this book.

Postcards are always hard to date and those reproduced here are particularly difficult. Where an exact date is given this is a best-guess based on a study of the card and its publisher. Other cards have been dated more broadly by the decade in which they were produced.

The text describing what is shown on the postcards is based on contemporary accounts of how china and earthenware were made and on discussion with those more knowledgeable than myself about the industry. Practice could vary from one potbank to another as well as changing over a period of years.

The photographs on pages 5, 21, 45, 47, 51, 54, and 63 are reproduced by kind permission of Royal Doulton, the copyright owner and proprietor of the Shelley trademark. This publication has been reproduced independently and neither I nor the publisher has any connection with Royal Doulton.

In putting the book together I have been helped by many who have shared their knowledge with me. I am particularly grateful to Mr Charles Dean for helpful comment. To all those who have added to my knowledge I record my grateful thanks. They have made writing this book a journey of discovery and pleasure. I hope those who read it will share this with me.

Roy Lewis

ETRURIA WORKS, *from the West.*

MANUFACTURE OF WEDGWOOD POTTERY

ETRURIA, 1902

When Josiah Wedgwood built the Etruria works in 1769 it was the largest potbank in the world. The original plan was based on two hollow squares, one producing useful ware and the other decorative ware. Over the years buildings were added piecemeal until the works looked like this in 1902. Wedgwood chose the name Etruria because it had been the homeland of the Etruscans who had produced fine pottery in ancient times.

GRINDING MILL AND YARD, TWYFORD'S, 1900

Twyford's Ltd built the Cliffe Vale Works at Hanley in the 1880s. Steam power was used to grind flint and cornish stone to be added to clay for their white earthenware. These raw materials were carried on the Trent and Mersey Canal, just visible on the right, and allowed to weather in the yard. The picture above shows boulders of cornish stone waiting to be crushed and ground. Note the crane needed to move the heaviest stones.

The Petters' Mill.

Preparing Materials for the Clay

Roma Series

MANUFACTURE OF WEDGWOOD POTTERY

THE FLINT MILL, WEDGWOOD, 1902

Flint was first calcined to make it whiter and more brittle and then crushed under heavy stampers. Afterwards it was ground very fine in a mill like the one shown on this postcard. The flint was shovelled into the large round pans seen above, each of which had four rotating arms which pushed round heavy stone boulders. The flint was ground between the boulders and the floor made of very hard stone. The pans were partly filled with water to reduce dust and allow the ground flint to be drawn off.

THE CHARM OF MERRY ENGLAND! 312-1.

A MARL HOLE, 1920

Marl or clay dug locally had once been used by all North Staffordshire potters. By 1920 its use was confined to some kinds of earthenware. Marl holes like the one above could be found behind the houses in parts of the Potteries. In the centre of the postcard can be seen the tracks up which waggons loaded with clay were pulled. When all the clay was used the hole would be filled with broken pots and cinders before being built over.

MIXING SLIP, SHELLEY POTTERIES, 1950s

China is made from a mixture of bone ash, china clay, and stone. The ingredients are ground very finely and then mixed with water in the correct proportions. By the 1950s, when this picture was published, this was done in large rotary cylinders like the one on the right. The resulting liquid is the consistency of cream and is called 'slip' The slip is passed over sieves of increasing fineness and under magnets (top left) to remove metal specks which would show in the finished china.

A SLIP HOUSE, 1910

In the slip house wooden trays, each with a cloth folded into a bag and fitted with a brass nozzle, are piled into stacks. When the men in this postcard had folded all the cloths, they would connect the nozzles to the pipe seen in the picture. Slip would then be pumped through the pipe into the bags. The surplus water is squeezed out by the pressure leaving a cake of clay. This is rolled up for the pug mill.

THE PUG MILL AT ETRURIA, 1920s

The pug mill is like a large sausage making machine. Rolls of clay from the slip house are fed in at one end. Inside, knives on a screw cut and knead the clay until all the air is removed and the clay is perfectly smooth. It is then squeezed out the other end in a long square sausage. The man on the right is cutting this into convenient lengths with a wire.

Neg: by Blake, Stationer, Longton.

II, "CLAY WEDGER", who kneads the clay to consistency.

THE CLAY WEDGER, 1904

Wedging was a laborious process. The worker lifted a lump of clay as it came from the slip house and threw it down on a hard surface to free it from air. This had to be repeated several times. After the introduction of the pug mill wedging was no longer necessary except for special jobs.

THE POTTER AT HIS WHEEL, 1910

The thrower is traditionally the aristocrat of the potbank — the craftsman with most skill in his hands. He sits horseback fashion in front of a revolving wheel, takes a ball of soft clay, throws it down on his wheel, raises it into a cone with his fingers and presses it down again until he is satisfied that the clay is just right. He then opens it out with his thumbs in the middle, pulls it up, and finishes the shape with one hand inside and the other outside the ware.

POTTER AT THE WHEEL IN HIS 80th YEAR. MAKING VASES

IE POTTER'S WHEEL.

THE OLD POTTERS' WHEEL, 1902

By the early twentieth century the potters' wheel was belt driven from a steam engine. In earlier times each wheel was turned by a vertical wheel which a woman turned at a steady speed. This photograph of an old fashioned wheel was taken by William Blake in April 1902 (there is a calendar on the wall) in a Longton potbank. The sign of E.J. Bloor's piano and organ warehouse in Stafford Street (now The Strand) can be seen through the window.

THE THROWER'S WHEEL, WEDGWOOD, 1902

When Etruria was built in 1769 Josiah Wedgwood himself threw the first vases in this workshop with his partner, Bentley, turning the vertical wheel for him. In this postcard of a later thrower at Etruria notice the stand by the side of the vase, holding a guide by which the size and shape of the vase can be checked.

Roma Series

MANUFACTURE OF WEDGWOOD POTTERY

The Thrower's Wheel

First Stage in Pottery Making

In this shop the famous Josiah Wedgwood formed the first vase made at Etruria, 1769, his partner Bentley turning the Wheel.

11

TURNING TEAPOTS, 1920s

After being thrown, pieces are allowed to dry until they are greenhard — the consistency of hard cheeses. They are then passed to the turner who uses a lathe similar to those used for working wood. He shaves the outside of the piece to a standard profile and then burnishes it with a steel tool. Some cast pieces are also turned. In this postcard the turner is checking the diameter of the hole at the top of a tea pot.

Neg.: by Blake, Stationer, Longton.

VII. Turning Cups on a Lathe.

TURNING CUPS, 1904

The lathe on this 1904 postcard is turned by a cord which also passes round a large wheel below the level of the work bench. The turner's assistant makes the wheel revolve with a treadle, like an old fashioned sewing machine. In the picture above, she is using her hand as a brake on the lathe. By 1904 treadles had been replaced by steam power in all the larger potbanks.

POTTERS MOULD MAKERS.

MOULD MAKERS, 1910

Throwing was a slow process. Large scale production was possible if pieces were cast. A model of the piece was made and this was used to produce dozens of moulds. The mould maker took the model, surrounded it with a wall or 'cottle' — a piece of old lino was sometimes used — and filled the space between the cottle and model with plaster of paris. When this had set, the model was removed.

MAKING MOULDS, 1920s

The mould maker in this postcard is trimming the edge of the mould after removing the cottle. Ralph Daniel of Cobridge is credited with the discovery in the 1740s that, if a mould made from plaster of paris was filled with slip, the mould would absorb surplus water leaving a coating of clay on the inside of the mould.

Neg: by Blake, Stationer, Longton.

VI. Casting Cups from liquid clay.

CASTING CUPS, 1904

The man on the left pours liquid clay or slip into a plaster of paris mould of a cup. When some of the water has been absorbed and a thick enough coating of clay deposited inside the mould, the surplus slip will be poured off. The assistant on the right will then take the mould to a heated drying room. When dry the clay shrinks away from the mould which can then be removed and re-used.

VIII. ATTACHING the Handles to Cups.

ATTACHING HANDLES TO CUPS, 1904

Handles were made by squeezing soft clay between two halves of a mould. In the middle of the nineteenth century this was done by young children who 'threw themselves on the mould and wriggled in a horizontal position, the moulds bearing forcibly on their chests.' In the postcard you can see how a handler took a cup in her left hand and a handle in her right. The ends of the handle were dipped in slip and this was enough to hold the handle in place when positioned on the cup.

THE DOD BOX, WEDGWOOD, 1920s

The dod box was an iron cylinder filled with soft clay. When the top was screwed down, a long ribbon of clay was forced out through a hole in the base — as in the picture on the left. The workman cut the clay ribbon into lengths which he bent into handles. After the handles had been dried, the ends were trimmed.

ATTACHING HANDLES TO JUGS, 1910

The jugs seen in the postcard above seem to have lids which the boy is removing from moulds and laying out. The two men are attaching handles to the jugs with slip. A pile of handles can be seen in the foreground.

THE CASTER, WEDGWOOD, 1920s
Pieces which are oval or a fancy shape cannot be thrown on a wheel and are cast in moulds. In this picture, taken at Etruria in the 1920s, a workman is carefully pouring slip into a mould for such a shaped piece.

REMOVING A MOULD,
SHELLEY POTTERIES, 1950s

Pieces with shapes like the one in this picture — probably the body of a coffee pot — have to be cast in moulds with several pieces. This postcard, taken at the Foley Works in Fenton, shows a four part mould. The raised projections fit into corresponding hollows to ensure an exact fit when the parts of the mould are put together.

THE PRESSER, WEDGWOOD, 1920s

Instead of pouring slip into a mould this workman has laid flat pieces of clay on each part of the mould and pressed them down firmly. When the mould has been assembled the seams are made good by putting a hand inside the piece. On this postcard the presser has removed part of the mould and is about to finish the outside by hand to ensure that there is no weakness on the seams.

MAKING 'TWYFORDS', 1900

Thomas Twyford designed the first one piece earthenware w.c. pan in the 1880s. Clay had to be pressed thickly inside large moulds made of wood and plaster of paris. His workmen were unused to such large and complicated moulds and there were also difficulties firing the pans. The manufacture was only perfected after several years of experiment. This picture shows 'Twyfords' being made in moulds at Cliffe Vale Works in 1900.

MAKING PLATES, 1904

This postcard shows a workman making plates upside down on a jigger or horizontal wheel. He has pressed soft clay over a plaster mould placed on the jigger in order to shape the upper surface of the plate. He is now using a specially shaped tool brought down on the clay while it is rotating. This squeezes the clay to the proper thickness and shapes the underside of the plate. Both plate and mould will then be placed in a hot room to dry.

MAKING BASINS, 1910

The workman shown on this postcard is making a large 'basin' inside a mould. He has covered the inside with soft clay and pressed it into every contour. He is now about to shape the inside of the basin by lowering the arm of the machine into the exact centre and making it rotate. The profile of the inside of the basin can be see on the arm.

Making Basins

WAR ON GERMANY.— MAKING DOLLS HEADS IN THE POTTERIES.

MAKING DOLLS HEADS, 1914

Before 1914 almost all china dolls' heads were made in Germany. The outbreak of war in 1914 provided an opportunity for Staffordshire potters to capture this market. The heads were cast in moulds and then trimmed by hand as can be seen in the postcard above. After they were fired they had to be painted (see opposite page) before being sent to the doll manufacturers.

COLOURING DOLLS HEADS, 1914

This photograph and the one on the opposite page were taken by William Blake of Longton, probably at Hewitt & Leadbetter's Willow Pottery, Longton. The company began making dolls heads in September 1914. The Staffordshire Advertiser reported, 'one of the largest firms of London buyers has placed an order for 10,000 for Christmas'. Very soon other North Staffordshire firms, like The Potteries Toy Company, also began to turn out dolls heads.

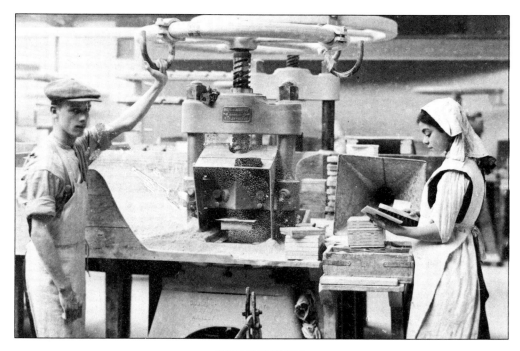

TILE PRESSING

From 1842 Mintons were using presses on the same principle as the one shown above to make floor tiles between metal dies. Clay dust was put into the lower die and compressed by a differential screw until it solidified. A pattern could be stamped into the tile at the same time and filled with clay of a different colour before firing and glazing. Floor tiles like these were immensely popular in the late nineteenth and early twentieth centuries because they were hard wearing and easily cleaned.

The "Figurers" Workroom
Relief Ornamenting of Jasper Ware
Tradition asserts that Flaxman modelled for Wedgwo
in this Shop more than a Century ago.

Roma Series

MANUFACTURE OF WEDGWOOD POTTERY

THE FIGURER'S WORK-ROOM, WEDGWOOD, 1902

In 1774 Josiah Wedgwood perfected jasper ware. Pieces were made from a clay body which would 'receive colours throughout its substance'. On to this blue, green or lilac background finely modelled white decoration was applied in relief. One of the original designers of the relief ornaments was John Flaxman, a famous sculptor, who worked in the room shown on this postcard.

FIGURE MAKING, WEDGWOOD, 1920s

Relief ornaments for jasper ware are made in plaster moulds. This postcard shows a young woman pressing soft clay into a set of shallow, open moulds. Surplus clay will be scraped off and the delicate leaves, scrolls, or figures turned out. The girl on page 29 is doing the same job in 1904 and visitors to the Wedgwood Visitors Centre at Barlaston can watch the same process being carried out today.

THE FIGURER, WEDGWOOD, 1920s

The figurer takes a piece of greenhard ware that has been turned. Then he carefully positions the soft clay relief ornament on it. Water and delicate pressure to make sure no air is trapped between the two clay surfaces are all that are needed to make the ornament adhere to the piece.

SAGGAR MAKING, 1914

Saggars are fireclay boxes in which the ware is placed during firing in the kiln. The word is a corruption of Safeguard, because the saggar safeguards the ware from dirt and smoke during firing. The man on the left has filled a rectangular frame with clay which he is beating out to the correct thickness for the sides of the saggar. The man on the right is doing the same for the saggar's base.

FINISHING A SAGGAR, 1914
This postcard shows the base and sides
of the saggar being put together before it
is fired. Although it was published by
William Shaw of Burslem about 1926,
the original photograph had been taken
by William Blake of Longton in 1914 at
the same time as the one on page 32.

Finishing a Sagger.

PLACING THE WARE IN SAGGERS READY FOR FIREING.

PLACING THE WARE IN SAGGARS, 1910

Most pieces ready for their first firing were quite dry and unlikely to stick together so that it did not matter if they touched each other when placed in saggars. Each pile of plates or saucers was bedded in flint dust so that the lowest piece was supported and less likely to lose shape. Cups might be stacked two deep with the top row upside down but practice varied from one potbank to another.

BISCUIT OVENS AT TWYFORD'S, 1900

The ovens where ware is given its first firing are called biscuit ovens and after being fired the pieces are biscuit ware. The ovens were circular coal fired furnaces with fireholes round the circumference. The fireholes led upwards inside the oven's domed roof and downwards through channels under the floor so that during firing the heat was evenly distributed. The oven was built inside a bottle shaped 'hovel' which sheltered it and provided a chimney to draw off smoke.

JOSIAH WEDGWOOD & SONS, LTD.

ETRURIA, Stoke-on-Trent

England

The "Oven"

A GLIMPSE at the inside of the Oven, where the ware is fired, showing how the "saggars" are built up in "bungs."

THE OVEN, WEDGWOOD, 1920s

This postcard shows how saggars filled with pieces of ware are stacked in the biscuit oven in columns called 'bungs'. The placer, who is responsible for seeing that the oven is properly filled, uses a ladder called a 'horse' to place the saggars at the top of each bung. When the oven is completely filled the entrance is closed with firebricks and a fire lit beneath the oven.

OVENS WHERE THE CLAY IS BAKED, 1904

Firing an oven takes from 30 hours upwards, according to the heat required by the ware in it, and cooling takes a similar time. In mid-nineteenth century when a bank was busy ovens were sometimes emptied while hot to save time. A workman wrote, 'The oven is so hot that if a man enters it his breath is almost taken away. His ears smart; he feels as if his nostrils are bleeding and as though his eyesight is almost gone from him on account of being in such a hot place'.

Photo by J. W. B. Blake Longton. — Potter's Series.

IX "OVENS" where the clay is baked.

THE KILNS.
WHERE THE WARE IS FIRED.

KILNS WHERE THE WARE IS FIRED, 1910

In addition to bottle ovens every potbank had a variety of other ovens and kilns. These were used for firing pieces at different stages in their manufacture. This postcard shows part of a bottle oven on the far right and two other kilns in the centre. In the foreground the photographer has posed a workman carrying two empty saggars, a man with a board of cups and three men filling a barrow with coal for the oven.

PLACING WARE IN KILNS, 1920s

The ware on the right is stacked awaiting the next stage in its manufacture — probably dipping (page 47–8). The plates on the left have already been decorated and are carefully kept apart so that the decoration will not be damaged before they are placed in the enamel kiln seen in the background (see page 62). The cups, carried on a board in the traditional way, are also ready to be placed in the kiln.

A WHIFF FROM THE POTTERIES, 1914

At the beginning of this century Stoke-on-Trent was said to be the smokiest town in Britain because of its coal fired bottle ovens. In the words of one writer, 'When firing was in progress dense black smoke came from the oven in considerable volume but without much force so that it hung in the lower air. Each of 300 potbanks had from three to a score of ovens so that the atmosphere was permanently filthy and a fog an appalling experience.'

STOKE-ON-TRENT AIR SOOTS ME WELL, 1939

In the early twentieth century trials were made with gas and, later, electrically heated ovens. These allowed better control of heat and gave off no smoke. Few potbanks made the change. In 1939, when this postcard was published, there were still 2,000 coal fired ovens and only 77 using gas or electricity. After the war change was more rapid. In June 1958 The Clean Air Act was applied to Stoke-on-Trent and by 1964 there were only 30 coal fired ovens left.

General View of Potteries.

SOMEWHERE THE SUN IS SHINING BUT NOT IN THE POTTERIES.

SOMEWHERE THE SUN IS SHINING, BUT NOT IN THE POTTERIES, 1912

Not all the smoke came from bottle ovens. Potbanks had chimney stacks for boilers that provided power for machinery and heated drying rooms. Houses had open coal fires and many Stoke housewives lit them even on summer evenings. A visitor in 1961 wrote, 'I heard it rumoured that a smokeless zone is to be decreed in Stoke-on-Trent. I should say that this would be the most unrealistic enterprise since American prohibition.'

Fresh Air from the Potteries.

FRESH AIR FROM THE POTTERIES, 1904

William Blake photographed some of the notorious smoky scenes and published them in 1904 as postcards with humorous titles like the one above. This view can be identified as Longton by the church tower on the left. Other titles include, 'O Beautiful, My Country!' and 'A bit thick for Father Christmas'. Blake's photographs were being reprinted by Shaws (Wolstanton) Ltd as late as the 1950s. The idea of 'smokies' was copied by other postcard publishers (see pages 4, 41, 42).

X. "SCOURERS" who remove dust before glazing.

SCOURERS, 1904

When ware was given its first firing in saggars it was bedded in pulverised flint dust to help it retain its shape. After firing, any of this dust which had adhered to the pieces had to be removed before the ware was glazed. This 1904 card shows women scouring it off with sandpaper and brushes. Particles of flint dust, if inhaled, could cause coughing, asthma and 'potters' rot'. The wooden screens and protective clothing were designed to reduce the risk to health.

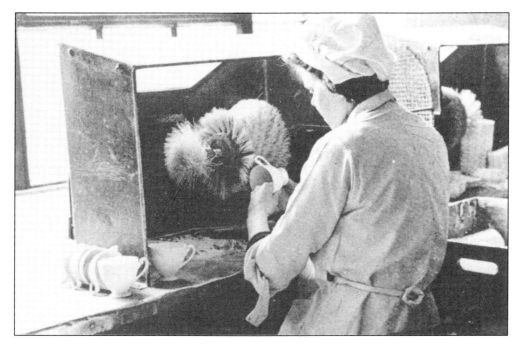

THE BRUSHING MACHINE, SHELLEY POTTERIES, 1950s

In the 1930s pulverised flint in the saggars was gradually replaced by alumina which was less of a health risk. In 1947 the use of flint was banned. When this picture was taken in the 1950s potbanks had introduced electrical brushing machines and extractor fans but protective clothing was still necessary.

RUNNING OUT A POTTERS FRIT KILN, 1937

After being brushed the biscuit ware, which is porous, is dipped in glaze to give it a non-porous coating. The glaze is a mixture of flint, borax and lead heated in a frit kiln, like the one above, until the ingredients are fused into a kind of glass. This is run out into a shallow pan. The glass is then ground very finely and mixed with water to make the glaze.

THE DIPPER, SHELLEY POTTERIES, 1950s

The text on this postcard published by Shelley Potteries explains, 'The dipper takes each piece of biscuit ware, immerses it in the tub of liquid glaze, and with a peculiar twist of the hand, removes any surplus and spreads it evenly over the surface It takes years to get that twist perfect.' The pieces are then placed separately on the board seen in the foreground to dry.

Dipping and Glazing the Ware.

DIPPING AND GLAZING THE WARE, 1910

Lead poisoning became a notifiable disease in the 1890s and after that the amount of lead in the glaze was reduced. However, powdered lead was still being used in 1910 and dipping was recognised as one of the most unhealthy jobs on the potbank. Workers' hands were always covered in glaze and their clothes became saturated as they worked. Wages had to be raised to persuade men to accept the risk to health. The use of lead in glaze was not banned until 1947.

Earthenware Dippers.

EARTHENWARE DIPPERS, 1914

Undecorated plates waiting to be glazed would not stick together so they could be stacked like those on the right in this postcard. Those which had been decorated while still in a biscuit state, like the one being held up by the man on the left, had to be stacked in pairs so that the decoration did not rub while awaiting glazing.

After glazing all pieces had to be separated until dry to avoid them sticking together.

JOSIAH WEDGWOOD & SONS, LTD.

ETRURIA, Stoke-on-Trent

England

Ware "placed" ready for the Glost Oven.

NOTICE the way the "saddles" and "thimbles" are used.

THE GLOST OVEN, WEDGWOOD, 1920s

After dipping, ware was fired in a glost oven where the glaze was fused into an impervious, clear, glass surface. Pieces had to be placed in saggars in such a way that they were kept apart and did not stick to each other when the glaze fused. The postcard shows how some of the specially shaped 'stilts', 'saddles', 'thimbles', and 'cockspurs' were used in saggars. All had very fine points which barely touched the pieces while separating them from each other.

GLOST PLACERS AT WORK, SHELLEY POTTERIES, 1950s

In the 1950s coal fired glost ovens were being replaced by electric tunnel ovens, like the one shown above at Shelley Potteries. The oven worked continuously. Pieces were placed between the shelves of a succession of trucks, like the one seen above, which travelled slowly through the heated tunnel, reaching a temperature of over 1000°C. The 140 foot journey through the tunnel took 30 hours.

Printing designs to decorate the Ware.

PRINTING DESIGNS, 1910

Pieces can be decorated either before or after they are glazed. Pre-glaze decoration was usually applied by a transfer. The design was first engraved on a copper plate. This postcard shows how oily colour was then pressed into the incised lines of the design with a wooden 'muller'. When all the lines had been filled with colour any surplus was scraped off with a palette knife (see page 53).

A POTTERS' PRINTER, 1914

The copper plate loaded with colour was covered with a sheet of very thin paper which had been brushed over with size. It was then placed on the press. The large lever, which can be seen behind the press on this postcard, was pulled down and the engraved copper plate slid under the roller and out again. The paper picked up colour from the incised lines and the design was printed. The woman on page 52 is holding up a transfer just off the press.

THE TRANSFERER, SHELLEY POTTERIES, 1950s

After the transfer sheet has been cut into sections, the transferer carefully places each one on the ware, making sure it is positioned in exactly the right place. A quick rub down with the brush whose handle can be seen on the right of this postcard and the design is transferred to the piece. The paper is easily removed when wetted. The piece is then put into a kiln on a low heat to drive off the oil in the colour before the piece is glazed.

THE PRINT ROOM, TWYFORD'S, 1900

At the beginning of the twentieth century it was fashionable to decorate sanitary ware with transfers. This picture shows some of Twyford's ware in their print room at the Cliffe Vale Works. The Gladstone Pottery Museum at Longton has a number of examples of sanitary ware decorated with transfers.

SPRAYING, 1906

Plain all-over colours were given to glazed pieces either by groundlaying — dabbing on colour — or by spraying. In this way no brush marks were left on the finished piece. This postcard, one of a set of six published by Raphael Tuck & Sons, shows a sprayer using her fore-finger to control the spray while the rest of her hand holds the colour reservoir.

DECORATING THE WARE, 1910

Designs were often outlined by a transfer and then filled in by paintresses like those shown at work on this postcard. The women 'have to be able to shade a petal so that the colour is deeper at the outer end and paint a bud $1/8$-inch across'. The work has always appealed to women. It is clean,gives scope for skill and neatness, and offers some variety with different patterns.

DECORATING CHINA.

DECORATING CHINA, 1914

The girl in the foreground is an apprentice being watched by the supervisor of the room. One woman recalled how, before 1914, young paintresses were treated as if in a very strict girls' school. No talking was allowed (although some supervisors let their girls sing hymns). Only one girl was allowed to go to the lavatory at a time. When such a request was made the supervisor would call, 'Is anyone out?'

A POTTERY ARTIST, 1930s

Paintresses were paid piecework and worked to a fixed design. Those potbanks which produced the finest ware also employed artists who painted freehand and were not under pressure of time. This postcard was published by Shaw of Burslem in the 1930s.

THE FINISHING TOUCHES, 1906
Decorated china was often finished off with a thin band of colour or gold. This postcard shows how the piece was placed on a wheel which the paintress controlled with her left hand while applying gold or colour with a camel hair brush held in her right. A very steady hand was required to keep the band even all the way round. Note the woman's lace trimmed overall.

FINISHING COTTAGE ORNAMENTS, 1906

Pairs of china dogs were among the most popular household ornaments in the early twentieth century. They were produced by a number of companies in the Potteries and this postcard shows a paintress at one of them adding the characteristic spots. Elsewhere on her table can be seen other ornamental animals and groups of figures.

AN ENAMEL KILN, WEDGWOOD, 1920s

Pieces which have been painted over the glaze have to be fired in an enamel kiln to fix the colours to the glaze. The temperature is much lower than in the glost oven, allowing a wide variety of colour to be used without being damaged by the heat. In this postcard you can see how pieces were placed on little stands on shelves in the kiln and not in saggars. These kilns were the first to be electrified. Josiah Wedgwood Ltd, for example, installed their first electric enamel kiln in 1927.

AN ELECTRIC ENAMEL KILN, SHELLEY POTTERIES, 1950s

This circular enamel kiln is electrically heated and continuous in operation. China is placed on the rotating platform which completes its journey round the kiln in 20 hours and reaches a temperature of 800°C. Notice how pieces are placed individually on the shelf or stacked in piles but carefully kept apart so that heat will reach all parts.

A CHINA WAREHOUSE, 1914-3

The warehouse was a busy place, as this postcard shows. Every pattern and every type of ware — cups, plates, dishes, etc — had its allotted place on the shelves. After inspecting each piece, one set of men placed the pieces on their proper shelves while others took pieces off the shelves to make up orders. Meanwhile, one man, seen here on the right, is keeping a record of which orders have been taken off the shelves.

PAPERING, 1914

Each order was made up in one or more baskets and taken to the paperers who wrapped each cup and small set of plates or saucers in tissue paper. The girl on this page is working at a bench with a young assistant to carry for her. The girls on the opposite page are working on their laps with baskets at their feet.

A WAREHOUSE, 1910

This postcard of sanitary ware in an unidentified warehouse was almost certainly taken at Longton about 1910. The dress of the men who posed for the photographer reflects their position in the works.

POTTERY PACKERS, 1914

China is fragile and unless it is carefully protected,cannot withstand the shocks and bumps it is likely to receive in transit. This postcard shows ware brought from the warehouse in wicker baskets being packed into chests and a barrel. The packer had to be an expert in the use of straw as a shock absorber.

PACKING CHINA, 1914

Much china was packed in large wicker crates like the ones shown on this postcard and on page 69. Crate making was a recognised trade in the Potteries up to the Second World War. After the war they were largely replaced by collapsible metal containers and cartons. In 1959 the President of the Pottery Manufacturers Federation forecast, 'In ten years time crates for packing pottery will be as out of date as bottle ovens.'

OUTSIDE THE PACKING SHEDS, TWYFORDS, 1900

In this víev of the yard outside the packing sheds at the Cliffe Vale Works the railway siding that ran into the works can be seen on the left. On the right are horse drawn drays loaded with crates of sanitary ware packed in straw. Many crates were loaded onto narrowboats on the nearby Trent and Mersey Canal. In 1900 over 50,000 tons of china and earthenware were sent from the Potteries by canal to Runcorn and then by lighter to Liverpool Docks.

MINTON'S DINNER HOUR, STOKE, 1904

Thomas Minton, a transfer-print engraver who is said to have invented the willow pattern, opened a small potbank in Stoke-upon-Trent in the 1790s. After he died, his son Herbert extended the works and Herbert's nephew, Colin Minton Campbell, further enlarged them. The works have now been rebuilt but are still on the same site in Campbell Place, where this picture was taken. The statue of Colin Campbell, MP, and Chairman of the North Staffordshire Railway, in the distance.

BROWN-WESTHEAD'S DINNER HOUR, 1904

This view shows Cauldon Place, Hanley, with Brown-Westhead, Moore & Co's works in the background and workers leaving for their dinner hour. Brown-Westhead, Moore & Co were china manufacturers, 'Potters to HM Queen Victoria by Special Appointment', with showrooms in London, Paris, Hamburg and New York. In 1905, the year after this postcard was published, the name of the company was changed to Cauldon Ltd and, later, to Cauldon Potteries Ltd.

A POTTERIES PRODIGY.

THE JUVENILE POTTER.
A British Clayworker with a display of her handiwork.
MISS EVELYN BAILEY.
52, CHURCH STREET. HANLEY.

MISS EVELYN BAILEY, late 1920s
The Stoke-on-Trent Education Committee developed Schools of Art in Burslem, Hanley, Longton and Stoke to provide training in pottery decoration, enamelling, gilding, modelling and design for young workers. This postcard, which probably dates from the late 1920s , shows one pupil, Miss Evelyn Bailey of Hanley, and her work. Does anyone know why she was honoured with a postcard of her own and how her career developed?